A Practical Guide to Getting
Out of the Funk You Are In With
Your Health, Mindset & Purpose

What the Funk?!

MOLLY SMITH

ISBN: 978-1-964619-84-2

Dedication

To Grayson and Graham:

Many of the stories and lessons in this book come from my journey of chasing society's definition of success and searching for my self-worth in all the wrong places. That search happened during some of the most important years of your lives. While I can't reclaim that precious time, my hope is that *when*, not if, you find yourselves feeling stuck or in a funk, you'll come back to this book and see how your mom found her way through. And always remember:

I love you.
I'm proud of you.
I always have your back.

Table of Contents

Foreword

It is an honor to write the foreword for Molly Smith's remarkable book, "What the Funk?! A Practical Guide to Getting Out of the Funk You Are in with Your Health, Mindset & Purpose." As someone who has walked a parallel path of self-discovery and transformation, I am inspired by Molly's story of resilience, honesty, and determination. Her journey, much like my own, is a testament to the power of aligning one's life with core values and purpose.

In March of 2023, Molly faced a defining moment in her career, expressing a raw vulnerability that many of us can relate to. Her courage to admit misalignment in her professional role and to take steps towards realignment is a powerful example of living authentically. It is in these moments of truth that we find our greatest strengths and the path to our true calling.

Molly's decision to eliminate alcohol from her life and confront her imposter syndrome head-on was a transformative step that sparked a cascade of positive changes. Her story underscores an essential truth: when we align our actions with our values, we unlock our full potential and create a ripple effect of positive change in our lives and the lives of those around us. This is a journey I deeply resonate with, having made similar choices in my own life to live congruently and purposefully.

Living in alignment, as Molly so eloquently puts it, is about self-awareness, authenticity, and growth. It is about saying yes to what fuels our passion and no to what drains our spirit. It is a journey, not a destination, and one that requires constant reevaluation and courage. Molly's insights into living aligned with purpose, mindset, and health offer practical guidance for anyone looking to make meaningful changes in their life.

Molly's practical steps to getting out of a funk in one's purpose, mindset, and health are not just theoretical but tried and tested. Her approach is holistic, recognizing that true fulfillment comes from addressing all aspects of our lives. Her story is a beacon of hope for those feeling stuck or out of alignment, showing that with each decision to live authentically, we move closer to our true selves.

As you dive into this book, I encourage you to embrace Molly's wisdom and let it guide you towards living a more aligned, fulfilling life. Her journey is a powerful reminder that we all have the strength within us to overcome our challenges and create the life we truly desire.

Thank you, Molly, for sharing your story and for inspiring us to live harder than life.

With gratitude and admiration,
Kelly Siegel-
Author of *"Harder than Life"* and Host of the *"Harder than Life Podcast"*

Acknowledgments

I'm incredibly grateful for the chance to share what I've learned—often through hard lessons—over the past five-plus years. There's a saying that's always stayed with me: "Our place of pain is our place of reign." I've come to believe that no pain or circumstance is ever wasted; every struggle has a purpose. Often, it's the people who step into our lives during those challenging times who help shape our future. So, I want to take this moment to recognize and thank those who have supported my journey and made the writing of this book possible.

To my amazingly patient husband, Geoff: Thank you for always supporting my dreams and letting me keep chasing what's next. I'm so grateful to share this life with you. Buckle up, cause I'm just getting started!

To Jen, Mom, Bob, Dad & Ellen: Thank you for being my biggest supporters. And Dad, the number you're looking for is 700 (I double checked).

To my besties and the Saturday morning crew: Thank you for holding space for me in the midst of figuring out how to write a book and keep doing all the other things on my plate. You've helped me stay grounded in this process and I'm so grateful for each of you.

To Lena and Avis: Thank you for guiding me through this season of leveling up, helping me trust my gut, and encouraging me to step confidently into what's next.

To Rob, Andre and Joe: I'm incredibly grateful for how we navigated my pivot in 2023. Standing on the edge of that life-changing shift was both thrilling and daunting, and your support and leadership made all the difference.

To my health community: Thank you for showing me what it means to partner with people with the *sole purpose of seeing them win*. I learned how to be a coach because of the example so many who have gone before have set.

To Dan & Megan Valentine and Doug & Thea Wood: Thank you for introducing the concept of "living congruently" and demonstrating how it's lived out each and every day. This concept has changed my life and is the basis for this book.

To the She Rises Studios Team: Thank you for the opportunity to share my story with the hope of inspiring others. Your support and guidance throughout the writing and publishing process have been truly invaluable.

Introduction

Have you ever felt like you're just going through the motions? That out-of-sorts feeling where life looks fine on the outside, but deep down, you know you were made for more? It's that nagging sense in your gut telling you that this—whatever "this" is—just isn't it. Life has a way of planting stories and thoughts in our minds that shape how we see ourselves and the world. We accept them as truth and act accordingly. Then one day, we wake up. For me, that day came in my mid-40s, and I realized that if anything was going to change, it was up to me to make it happen.

In 2019, I found myself at a crossroads. On paper, everything was going well. My career was thriving, I was climbing the corporate ladder, and the coveted C-level role felt within reach. I poured my energy into work, driven by ambition and the belief that success in business equaled worth. I was fortunate to have (and still have) a supportive husband who stepped up at home and with our boys so I could chase my goals. But even with all of that, there was a problem I couldn't ignore—my physical health was in the proverbial toilet. I was obese, uncomfortable in my own skin, and dealing with a list of medical conditions tied to poor habits. What made it worse was that I didn't believe I could change it. And that's when I knew: *I was in a funk.*

This was the start of my journey to pivot out of that funk and reclaim my life.

At its core, *What the Funk?!* is an experiential guide about living in alignment with your true self—your real, authentic self that reflects your values and vision for the future. Now, I know "living in alignment" might sound a bit out there but let me break it down. Living in alignment, or congruently, is about shifting how you show up in life, especially when it comes to your health, mindset, and purpose. It means making choices that represent who you are and staying true to what matters most to you.

And let me tell you, when you start living in alignment with your true self, it's like unlocking a new level of freedom and purpose. The beauty of it is that this shift doesn't just impact you; it creates a ripple effect that inspires those around you. It breathes life into everything you touch, making positive changes not just in your own life, but in the lives of those you care about. Sound good? If it feels out of reach, hang in there. Because the moment you decide to pivot out of the funk, you've already taken the first step. Each step afterward builds momentum, and with each aligned decision, you'll feel more freedom and fulfillment. I won't sugarcoat it—it's deep, soul-searching work, but it's absolutely worth it.

Throughout the following chapters, I'll take you through some of my most vulnerable moments, like abandoning that daily glass (or three) of wine to unwind, struggling with the nagging feeling that I wasn't enough in my corporate role, and realizing that my coping mechanisms of doom scrolling and binge-watching Netflix were only keeping me stuck. Does any of that sound familiar?

Here's the thing: I've been in a funk more times than I can count. And here's what I now know—you can get out of it, and you can just as easily find yourself back in it. The good news here is the strategies I share in this book are tools you can use over and over again. For instance, when I find myself behind on my favorite personal development podcasts, it's a sign I'm out of alignment and potentially heading back into a funk. But now, I recognize it as a signal. I pause, run through the Mindset

Inventory™ (more on that in Part 2), check how I'm spending my downtime, and shift things before I'm too deep in the funk.

Each chapter wraps up with three guiding sections:

- *How do you know if you are in a funk?*
- *What does pursuing alignment look like?*
- *Your next best step*

These sections are here to help you pinpoint where you are and map out what to do next. Because sometimes, the thought of making changes can feel overwhelming enough to paralyze us. My goal is to break down the overwhelm and help you move into action toward a life that feels fulfilling, free, and full of joy.

So, let's dive in. This isn't just my story—it's a toolkit for you to step out of the funk and into a life of fulfillment, freedom and joy.

Part 1:
Alignment in your physical health

You've probably heard the saying, "If you don't make time for your health, you'll be forced to make time for your illness." It's one of those truths that hits harder the busier life gets. When we're overwhelmed, health often gets shoved to the back burner—but here's the thing: if you want to break free from a funk, your physical health is where it all starts.

Why? Because when your health is moving in the right direction, it creates a ripple effect. You're better equipped to navigate the other areas of your life—your mindset, your work, your relationships, and even how you show up day-to-day. Health isn't something you "check off the list." It's the foundation for everything else.

When our physical health is out of alignment, it feels like we're carrying extra weight—figuratively and sometimes, literally. Whether it's the joint pain, the "hangry" mood swings, or the constant cycle of starving and stuffing because meals are an afterthought, it all adds up. And it impacts how we feel, how we treat others, and how we move through the world.

That's why we're starting with physical health. This is where my own journey out of a funk began and let me tell you—I didn't do it perfectly. I've messed up more times than I can count, but what matters is creating habits that are sustainable. The goal isn't to "get it perfect"—it's to create momentum that makes it easier to keep going.

In this part of the book, I'm sharing what worked for me. From getting to a healthy weight and incorporating movement and to figuring out where alcohol fits in and tuning into what's happening "under the hood"—what I like to call your "healthy innards." This isn't about rigid rules or impossible standards; it's about building a foundation that supports your best self.

So, let's dive in. Together, we'll tackle what it means to get your health aligned in a way that fits your life and fuels the journey ahead.

Chapter 1

Keeping Your Innards Optimized

"Are you freaking kidding me?"

That was my immediate reaction when I read the message from my primary care doctor, casually suggesting we recheck my thyroid levels in six weeks. Let me back up—three weeks earlier, I had gone in for what I assumed was a routine "med check" to renew my thyroid prescription. Instead, based on my lab results, she decided to reduce my dosage.

Fast forward 10 days, and I was dragging myself through each afternoon, barely able to stay awake, my productivity in freefall. And, if you asked my husband, I'd apparently added "short-tempered" to my list of side effects. The thought of enduring this for six more weeks was just not an option. Who could function like that? Certainly not me—not with my never-ending to-do list.

But the worst part wasn't the fatigue or the mood swings—it was the hopelessness. What was I supposed to do for the next six weeks? Wait it out and hope for the best? It felt like I was trapped in a situation I couldn't control. Have you ever been in a position like this with a medical professional? It's confusing, frustrating, and honestly, a little scary.

Here's the thing: we can sit in that frustration, or we can take action. For a long time, I believed doctors had all the answers and blindly followed their advice. Don't get me wrong—I have an enormous amount of respect for the incredible work doctors do every day. But this particular experience reminded me of an important truth: while doctors are experts in their field, you are the expert on your body. No one else knows what it's like to live in your skin, feel what you feel, or experience the subtle shifts that signal something is off.

The more I thought about my experience, the more I realized it wasn't unique. In fact, it's part of a much larger trend in how we approach health. Consider this: nearly 70% of adults aged 40-79 take one or more prescription medications daily, according to the CDC. That's a staggering number, and it paints a clear picture of how many of us are managing symptoms without truly addressing the root causes.

On top of that, over 42% of adults are classified as obese—a statistic that comes with an increased risk of countless health conditions, from heart disease to diabetes. These aren't just numbers; they're red flags. They tell us that for too many of us, our health isn't as strong as it could be.

After receiving my primary care doctor's advice to wait it out for six weeks, I knew I couldn't sit by and hope for the best. A few days later, I stumbled across Dr. Jamie Gilliam, a functional medicine practitioner, on social media. Her videos on thyroid and hormone health were eye-opening. I didn't know much about functional medicine, but after a little research, I realized it was exactly what I needed.

Functional medicine feels like having a personalized health detective on your team. It's not about treating the symptoms but understanding the bigger picture—how lifestyle, nutrition, hormones, and genetics all play a role in your health. It's a tailored, comprehensive approach, not a one-size-fits-all solution.

For me, choosing functional medicine wasn't just about switching doctors. It was about taking ownership of my health and finding someone who would partner with me. Dr. Jamie didn't just review my thyroid labs; she asked about everything. It was like she was putting together a puzzle where every piece mattered.

Through comprehensive testing, Dr. Jamie uncovered that my thyroid was in fact severely under-medicated. But that wasn't all—there were other underlying issues, like inflammation, other hormonal imbalances and liver health, that needed attention. For the first time, I felt like someone truly saw the whole picture of my health.

She created a protocol tailored specifically to me: compounded thyroid medication, additional hormone support, holistic supplements, and—most importantly—education. She even taught me how to read my own labs and understand what optimal ranges looked like.

That education was a game-changer. I started to see my health differently—not as a collection of symptoms but as an interconnected system. Every choice I made, from what I ate to how I managed stress, played a role in how my body functioned.

Here's the thing: you can't fix what you don't understand. And you can't understand what you don't take the time to notice. For me, learning to tune in to my body's signals was the first step in getting my health back on track.

Think about it: how often do we ignore the little signs that something is off? The afternoon fatigue, the headaches that pop up out of nowhere, the extra weight that won't budge—these aren't just nuisances; they're your body's way of telling you it needs attention.

When we get curious about what's happening inside, we gain the power to make meaningful changes. It's not about obsessing over every detail but about developing an awareness of how your body feels and functions. That awareness can be the difference between living with chronic issues and taking control of your health.

These stats and stories aren't meant to scare you. They're here to empower you. By recognizing the signs, asking the right questions, and making informed decisions, you can transform your health—not just for today but for the long haul.

How do you know if you are in a funk?

Before you can take steps to improve your health, you need to recognize when something's off. Often, we normalize feeling tired, foggy, or stressed because life is busy—but your body has a way of sending signals when it's out of alignment.

Start by taking a closer look at your physical, mental, and emotional well-being. Are there signs that things aren't quite right? Here are a few common cues:

- **Physical Symptoms:** Unexplained aches and pains, digestive discomfort, sleep disruptions, or changes in appetite.

- **Mental Symptoms:** Trouble concentrating, forgetfulness, or persistent brain fog.

- **Emotional Symptoms:** Feeling unusually irritable, anxious, or down, even when there's no clear reason.

These aren't just minor inconveniences—they're your body's way of saying, "Hey, something needs attention." Learning to identify and listen to these signals is the first step toward getting out of a funk.

What does pursuing alignment look like?

Pursuing alignment is about more than just ticking off boxes on a to-do list; it's about creating a personalized approach to your health that works for you.

Here's what that can look like:

- **Advocating for Your Needs**: This means finding a medical practitioner who listens to your concerns and respects your input. It's not about blindly following advice—it's about creating a partnership where your voice matters.

- **Educating Yourself**: Learn to ask questions, research your symptoms, and understand the basics of your lab results. The more informed you are, the more empowered you'll feel to make decisions that align with your unique needs.

- **Tuning In to Your Body**: Alignment begins with awareness. Pay attention to how your body feels after meals, during stressful times, or at the end of a long day. Small adjustments based on these observations can lead to big changes over time.

Pursuing alignment isn't a one-and-done process. It's an ongoing journey of refining, learning, and making adjustments as you go.

Your next best step:

If you're ready to take the first step toward getting your "innards" healthy, here's a simple roadmap to get started:

1. **Get a Baseline**: Schedule a visit with your doctor to check your current health stats. Request lab work that goes beyond the basics - ask for a comprehensive lab panel that provides a *full*

picture of your health, helping to identify any imbalances or underlying issues.

2. **Learn the Difference**: Research the difference between standard and optimal lab ranges. Functional medicine often looks at narrower, optimal ranges to catch issues earlier and fine-tune your health.

3. **Track What You Notice**: Keep a journal for a week or two. Write down how you feel physically, mentally, and emotionally throughout the day. Tracking these details can uncover patterns that give you insight into what's going on inside.

4. **Explore Your Options**: If you're not getting the answers you need from your current healthcare provider, consider seeking a functional or integrative medicine practitioner. A second opinion can open the door to new possibilities.

You don't need to have all the answers right away. The key is to start somewhere—anywhere—and take that first step toward understanding what's going on inside.

Chapter 2

Feeling Good in Your Skin

There I was, standing in my closet in a red terry cloth robe, staring at my wardrobe. An all too familiar feeling of dread settled in the pit of my stomach. I hated getting dressed every day – not because I didn't like my clothes, but because everything was too tight. Just for once, I wanted to walk into my closet with confidence and pick out something that felt good. That made me feel good in my own skin. Have you felt this way?

Every morning, picking out what to wear to the office had turned into a soul-sucking ritual. On that particular morning, I opted for the *ever-so-reliable* stretchy black pants. I longed for a change and a departure from the perpetual dissatisfaction I felt in my own skin. No matter how hard I tried to lose the weight, I was trapped in a frustrating cycle of trying and failing over and over again.

In the previous four years, I had been grappling with an autoimmune condition that left my thyroid nonfunctional. High blood pressure and acid reflux had also joined the party, tethering me to daily medications. Juggling 60-70 hour workweeks in a demanding job while keeping up with an active family made losing weight feel impossible.

Evenings became my escape—the glass (or three) of pinot noir and playing a round of Candy Crush offered a brief moment of solace before a restless night's sleep. But the consequences of my unhealthy habits stared back at me every morning when I opened my closet.

Just when things felt their worst, a glimmer of hope appeared in my Facebook feed—thanks to my friend, Dee Ann. I had been following her remarkable weight loss journey from afar. She posted a side-by-side picture of where she started and where she was now—I couldn't believe it! She clearly was doing something that was working, and I wanted to know more, so I reached out to her. That call was a pivotal moment and my first step towards getting out of the funk with my weight.

"I work a lot of hours, I have two active kids, food prepping stresses me out, and I'm gluten intolerant. Will this work for me?" I inquired, laying bare the complexities of my life. She assured me that it would work for me, but I was scared of trying and failing again.

Clinging to Dee Ann's belief in me and this program, I decided to try it. The program she recommended involved eating six times a day and increasing my water intake. It was a structure I hadn't experienced before, but I decided to trust the process. By the fourth day, I knew something was different. Instead of opting for the typical Sunday afternoon nap, I was tackling household chores and getting things done. This burst of energy mid-afternoon was new. However, the most surprising part wasn't just the physical boost; it was how clear-headed I felt. I hadn't realized how sluggish my body and mind had become until I started fueling them consistently. The first week, I lost 5 pounds, my energy was great, and I was sleeping better than I had in years.

Week after week, I continued following the program, albeit not perfectly. The physical transformation was hard to miss as I was *literally shrinking*. I realized two key things set this journey apart from all my past attempts to lose weight—and surprisingly, it wasn't just about what I was eating or drinking.

When it comes to making big changes to your daily habits and routines—especially around health—trying to go it alone rarely works. We're hardwired for connection, and having the right support can make all the difference. It's not just about staying consistent; it's about truly transforming how we approach our health and habits. One of the most valuable aspects of the program I followed was the built-in support—a community of like-minded people and the guidance of a dedicated coach.

I heard James Clear, author of *Atomic Habits*, say that we need to "join tribes where the desired behavior is the normal behavior." This community was exactly that—a group of people all focused on improving their health, just like me. They weren't perfect, but they were committed, and that created an environment where healthy choices felt not only possible but expected. Sharing our journeys—our challenges, victories, and everything in between—helped me stay grounded in my own path. Being surrounded by others creating what I wanted to create gave me a sense of possibility and momentum that I couldn't have achieved on my own.

Then there was Dee Ann, my coach. She didn't just hand me the program and check out; she was my guide, cheerleader, and occasional voice of reason when I started to veer off track. When old habits crept in or I felt stuck, she helped me refocus and reminded me why I started in the first place. Her support was never about judgment—it was about accountability, encouragement, and equipping me with the tools to navigate the emotional hurdles that come with change.

Every other time I'd tried—and failed—to lose weight, I had done it on my own. A long day at work or a curveball on the home front would almost always derail me. I'd default to what was easy and convenient, even if it didn't align with what I truly wanted. Left to my own devices, it was too easy to break the commitment I'd made to myself.

This time was different. With the accountability of a coach and the shared energy of a community, the commitment I made to myself felt stronger—like I finally had the tools to follow through. If you're looking to make lasting changes to your physical health, especially your weight, here's the bottom line: *don't go it alone.*

While the support of a coach and community kept me on track, I realized that lasting change required more. I needed to understand my deeper reason for wanting to drop the weight. That's where my *why* came in.

Understanding the key driver behind making a change is crucial. What I've found is that people (me included) often start highly motivated— the excitement of a fresh start can carry you for a while. But motivation is fleeting, and when it fades, something deeper needs to take its place.

When I began my journey, my goal seemed straightforward: I wanted to fit into my clothes again and stop feeling so uncomfortable in my own skin. But as I stayed consistent with the program and started seeing real progress, I realized it wasn't just about the weight. My *why* wasn't tied to a number on the scale—it was tied to the life I was building. I wanted the freedom to move through life with confidence and the ability to say yes to opportunities I once believed were out of reach.

This deeper reason became my anchor. It grounded me on the tough days when motivation waned and willpower felt nonexistent. I quickly learned that motivation alone wasn't enough to sustain lasting change. Instead, it was the vision of the life I was working toward—the version of myself I was becoming—that kept me moving forward.

This wasn't about white knuckling it through cravings or tough moments. It was about aligning my daily choices with the bigger picture of the life I wanted. Each step I took wasn't just about what I was leaving behind—it was about moving closer to the life I was creating.

In hindsight, I see how everything was connected. The support of a coach, the encouragement of a community, and the clarity of my why were the threads that tied it all together. Change doesn't happen in isolation—it's the relationships we lean on and the vision we hold that turn fleeting effort into lasting transformation.

Oh, and that wardrobe that once filled me with dread? Every single piece had to be replaced—going from busting out of a size 16 to comfortably wearing a size 6 will do that. But the real transformation wasn't just in my closet or on the scale. It was in how I showed up in my day-to-day life—with confidence, energy, and a sense of purpose that finally matched the vision I had for myself.

How do you know if you are in a funk?

Whether my story resonates with you or not, there are some key indicators that might signal you're in a funk:

- Feeling uncomfortable in your own skin, like you don't recognize yourself anymore.
- Getting consistent reminders from your doctor about losing weight or improving your health.
- Realizing that none of your clothes fit the way they used to.
- Avoiding group photos—or placing yourself in the background—because you don't want to be seen.

Recognizing these signs is the first step in acknowledging that something needs to change. It's not about judgment—it's about awareness. Once you see it, you can start taking steps to address it.

What does pursuing alignment look like?

Here's the truth: you don't have to wait until you reach your "goal weight" to feel aligned. Alignment is found in the small, consistent actions that move you closer to a healthier, more energized version of yourself. It's in choosing water over soda, prepping meals for the week, or simply taking the stairs instead of the elevator. These choices may feel small in the moment, but they represent progress—and progress is what matters most.

Alignment in health also requires giving yourself grace. No one gets it right 100% of the time. Life happens, habits slip, and cravings hit. But pursuing alignment means focusing on the bigger picture: your dedication to returning to *habits that serve your goals*, even when things don't go perfectly. It's not about perfection; it's about *consistency*.

When you approach your health journey this way, the focus shifts from chasing an elusive end point to appreciating the growth and transformation happening along the way. You begin to celebrate the wins—both big and small. These victories remind you that the journey itself is valuable and worth honoring.

Your next best step:

All progress starts with telling the truth about where you are right now. Take 3-4 days to record everything you eat and drink using a tool like MyFitnessPal or Cronometer. This isn't about being hard on yourself—it's about gaining clarity. Understanding how you're currently fueling your body is an important first step in making intentional changes. After all, you can't outrun your fork.

Navigating the path to a healthy weight on your own can be overwhelming, especially when life inevitably gets messy. That's why finding a program rooted in habit transformation, supported by a coach and a like-minded community, is essential. The right program not only provides structure but also gives you the accountability and encouragement you need to stay consistent, even when challenges arise. Having a team in your corner makes the journey feel less daunting and far more achievable.

To learn more about the program that helped me transform my health, email me at molly@mollypositivepants.com or visit www.nextbeststep.co.

Chapter 3
Breaking Free from the Alcohol Trap

As I scrolled through my Facebook feed on that chilly evening of January 31, 2023, the thought, *"What in the blazes is she doing?"* flashed through my mind. There, in the midst of the 20-degree weather, was my friend Jenny, standing outside in an electric blue bikini and robe. The recent winter storm had left a snowy blanket around her pool in North Texas, and she was live on Facebook, ready to plunge into the icy water. Intrigued, I unmuted her video to uncover the reason behind her polar plunge—and I quickly realized it wasn't just a wild stunt. Jenny was celebrating 100 days of living alcohol-free.

As she shared her journey, detailing her newfound clarity and the transformative impact of kicking alcohol to the curb, her words resonated with me deeply. I felt a pull to reconnect with her after a couple of years and couldn't resist sending her a message, eager to know more about what inspired her to embrace an alcohol-free lifestyle and how it had shifted her life in such a profound way.

Looking back, I know that Jenny's video showing up in my feed was divine intervention. During that last month, like clockwork, as soon as 5 p.m. hit, I found myself pouring a glass (or three) of wine from my extensive 90-bottle wine fridge. I convinced myself it was a way to "unwind from the daily grind," but beneath the surface, I knew the truth: I was using alcohol to escape. What I wasn't sharing openly was how suffocating feelings of inadequacy had taken over my professional life, making even my successes feel like flukes and convincing me it was only a matter of time before everyone saw I was in over my head.

Work had been a constant source of stress, with the demands of my job evolving over the 2.5 years I'd been there. I clung to my high standards, but as the landscape of my role shifted, I felt lost. By the time I wrapped up my day, I was exhausted, mentally and emotionally. All I wanted was to numb the feelings of not being smart enough, of falling short. That glass of wine was my temporary sanctuary—a quick way to silence the inner critic and create distance between me and the chaos in my head.

The truth was, I didn't have the tools to process or even feel those emotions. I wasn't managing them at all—I was numbing them. The wine had become my emotional escape hatch. But as I watched Jenny's Facebook live that night, I reached a breaking point. I was tired of living out of alignment with my values and pretending like I had it all together. Here I was, a health coach telling others to build healthy habits, and yet I was using alcohol to cope with my emotions. I was in a funk, no doubt about it. Jenny's video offered a glimpse of what life could look like on the other side, but while I was intrigued, I wasn't ready to commit just yet.

That evening, during a FaceTime call with my mentor, Remy, I finally admitted what I'd been avoiding: "Honestly, I'm not doing great. My health is in the tank, and I'm drinking every night." I shared Jenny's story with her and my plan to reach out. It was a raw moment where I acknowledged how incongruent my life had become. Remy encouraged me to go 100 days without drinking and refocus on my nutrition. Despite the gnawing fear of failure, I agreed to try.

I started my 100-day journey quietly. I didn't share it on social media, partly because I wasn't sure I'd stick to it, and I didn't want to fail publicly. This backfired when my closest girlfriends surprised me with an afternoon of wine tasting and painting for my birthday. I hadn't shared my commitment with them, and it made for an awkward moment. But even though we were at a winery, I stayed true to my commitment and found that I could still enjoy the day without the wine. Not surprisingly, my closest friends became my biggest supporters.

As the days went by, I began to feel the real benefits of cutting out alcohol. Better sleep and clearer mornings were just the start—I also noticed a shift in how I approached social situations. The belief that I needed wine to have a good time slowly lost its power over me. Sure, there were moments when I craved a perfect glass of pinot noir with dinner, but the trade-off no longer felt worth it. The fleeting "joy" of a few glasses inevitably turned into regret, restless nights, and sluggish mornings.

As I stepped further away from alcohol, I uncovered a deeper truth: I had been using it to avoid confronting difficult emotions. Without the tools to process my feelings, wine became *my escape*. Taking a break from drinking forced me to face those emotions head-on. It wasn't just about cutting out alcohol—it was about learning to navigate my emotions in a healthier, more constructive way.

Sobriety brought a clarity I hadn't experienced in years. Waking up with a clear mind and making intentional choices reminded me that joy doesn't come from a wine glass—it comes from *living authentically*. What started as a temporary experiment transformed into a lifestyle. With each passing day, alcohol loosened its grip, and I embraced the vitality and resilience that sobriety unlocked.

This journey wasn't just about giving up alcohol—it was about trusting myself and listening to the voice I had ignored for so long. What began as a single challenge became the foundation for a new way of living, defined by emotional clarity, freedom, and a deeper connection to what truly matters.

How do you know if you are in a funk?

Do you find yourself reaching for a glass of wine (or your drink of choice) each evening as a way to unwind? Maybe it's become your go-to way to relax after a long day. While it might feel like a quick fix, it's worth asking yourself if there are healthier ways to recharge that could leave you feeling more refreshed.

Have you ever woken up with a twinge of regret about how much you drank the night before? That uneasy feeling might be a sign that alcohol is playing a bigger role in your life than you'd like.

In social settings, does alcohol feel like a necessary ingredient for fun or connection? Using it to boost enjoyment or ease interactions might mean it's become a crutch rather than just a casual choice.

And what about those moments when life feels heavy or overwhelming—do you notice alcohol temporarily quieting the discomfort? While it might seem to help in the moment, relying on it this way could be masking deeper feelings that need your attention.

What does pursuing alignment look like?

If you resonated with any of the scenarios mentioned above, congratulations, you've already taken a significant step forward by acknowledging and increasing your awareness of how alcohol fits into your life. It's no small feat to confront the role alcohol plays and how it may be used as a crutch or coping mechanism. Taking an honest look at the circumstances and the emotions that drive the desire to drink can indeed feel like stepping into a whirlwind of overwhelming introspection. But rest assured, this discomfort is a sign of progress, indicating that you're on the right path towards understanding and change.

Now, if you're feeling overwhelmed by this newfound awareness, know that you're not alone. Know that these feelings will eventually subside as you navigate through them. It's essential to reach out and connect with others who have walked this path before you.

Your next best step:

Connect with people who have chosen to remove alcohol from their lives and ask about their experiences. Building a support network of others who are sober-curious or embracing an alcohol-free lifestyle can make a huge difference. It's tough to go it alone, and having like-minded individuals to lean on can provide both encouragement and accountability. You might also find inspiration by following people on social media, like Kelly Siegel, who share their journey and celebrate living a fulfilling, alcohol-free life. (His story was so impactful during my first 100 days and beyond, I asked him to write the foreword for this book!)

Chapter 4

Moving Beyond the Excuses

Between my sister Jen and me, she was undoubtedly the more active one in the family. From a young age and well into adulthood, Jen was deeply involved in various sports: soccer, softball, basketball and even a stint in women's professional football. As for me, well, let's just say I took a different route. I played softball for a brief moment at the age of 7 or 8, but my athletic career ended almost as quickly as it started. I wasn't a fan of running in the heat with the yellow and black uniforms with a big bee on it (sorry, Wild Honeys teammates). This early memory is the basis for the story that being active was too hard, exhausting or not worth my time. I never pursued sports or athletics again growing up.

It wasn't until almost four decades later that I started to change the deeply held belief that it was too hard, exhausting, or not worth my time.

Now, I could bombard you with all sorts of statistics about how important the role of exercise is in maintaining overall health, but that's not where my focus lies in this book. My goal is to assist you in getting out of the funk that holds you back from embracing activity and exercise. And trust me, it's infinitely more about shifting our *mindset* and *belief about ourselves* than simply getting our bodies moving.

When it comes to getting active, there are at least two distinct camps, and I've had my fair share of experiences in both. On one side, there's the belief that exercise is just too hard, we're too far gone, too busy and starting won't make a difference, leading many to never even attempt to start. The other camp on the opposite end of the spectrum, is a relentless pursuit of an *unrealistic ideal,* which often leaves us feeling defeated, overwhelmed and unmotivated.

It's Too Hard

Back when I was climbing up the corporate ladder, trying to squeeze in exercise seemed like a Herculean task. I'd tell myself I didn't have the time, but deep down, I just didn't see it as a priority. I had this belief that it wouldn't really make a difference anyway, and I was kind of clueless about what would actually help me reach my goals.

I'd make these short-lived attempts – hitting the gym in my office building for a week or two – but I could never stick with it long enough to make it a habit. It felt like I was caught in this frustrating cycle of starting and stopping, with no real progress to show for it. And each time I quit and ventured back towards my familiar sedentary life, it just reinforced this idea that I wasn't a physically active person, exercise was too much hassle, and any attempts would leave me feeling crappy about myself. Since my first foray into rec level softball, I let this mistaken idea take root in my mind: that getting active and exercising was just too hard, and it wasn't who I was. Instead, I gravitated towards the comfort of work, where I found my sense of worth and confidence.

This began to shift for me in 2019. I was 8 months into my weight loss journey, and I had already lost about 40 pounds. I had a newfound confidence that developed over the previous couple of months as I started to see significant changes in my health and mindset. I began to *believe* that I could do things that I never before thought were possible.

At a conference in Phoenix in October of 2019, I was challenged by Jon, one of the mentors in my health coaching business, to run a half marathon. The challenge was preposterous. I couldn't run from here to there without stopping and reaching for an oxygen tank to catch my breath. He began to walk through how I could do it, which included downloading a "couch to half" training app which would help me build endurance and skill so I could complete 13.1 miles on race day... which was 14 weeks later.

As I mulled over this challenge, I had a realization. I'd already *proven to myself* that I could do the seemingly impossible by shedding those 40 pounds that I had been holding onto for over a decade. So why not take on this half marathon challenge? Who says I can't? The only thing holding me back was, well, me. And that's when I made a decision. Right then and there, I signed up for the Cowtown Half Marathon in Ft. Worth on March 1, 2020 and downloaded a couch to half training app on my phone.

As I kicked off this 14-week journey, I realized right away that smooth sailing wasn't in the cards. It felt more like navigating a sea of doubt, uncertainty and procrastination. I mean, there were moments when I seriously questioned my own sanity, wondering if I'd bitten off more than I could chew. Every time I glanced at the training app and saw the progression of distances I was supposed to tackle, a wave of overwhelm crashed over me. It was *too hard*. It was a constant reminder of the nagging belief that exercise was just too difficult. But despite the inner resistance, I knew I had to keep pushing forward. So, I took my next best step, knowing full well that my efforts might not always sync up perfectly with the app's expectations. So I continued on... imperfectly.

Amidst the sweat, the struggles, and the moments of self-doubt, I had to *redefine* what success meant to me in the context of this race. It wasn't about hitting specific time goals or actually running all 13.1 miles; it was about crossing that finish line, no matter how long it took or what method I used to get there. So, I adjusted my expectations, embracing a mix of walk/run intervals to keep my endurance up and curating the ultimate Spotify playlist to keep my motivation levels soaring.

In the midst of it all – the sore muscles, the many setbacks, the self-doubt – I held onto the visualization of crossing the finish line. And on March 1, 2020, with my husband by my side, I crossed the finish line in 3 hours and 23 minutes. In the running world, this time is most unimpressive for a half marathon. In my world, I had just accomplished something I never thought possible. And more importantly, that deeply held narrative that "exercise was too hard" was shifting.

As I crossed the finish line and reflected on the past 14 weeks of less-than-perfect training, I could clearly see the growth in my self-belief. Each time I pushed myself out the door for a run, even when I didn't feel like it, I reinforced the notion that I am capable of tackling challenges head-on. It was clear that I had grown since beginning 14 weeks earlier. While the journey remained tough, the personal development that followed each difficult step made it all worthwhile.

Chasing an Unrealistic Ideal

On the flip side, pursuing an unrealistic ideal when it comes to exercise and being active can also leave us in a funk. I spend a lot of time with people who are pursuing optimal and ultra health and it's an amazing community to be a part of because we have a shared value of prioritizing our health. However, it's easy to get into *comparative reality*, which is a dangerous place to camp out. Theodore Roosevelt said that "comparison is the thief of joy" and I couldn't agree more!

I'm an advocate for setting big, hairy audacious goals, then breaking them down into manageable steps. However, as you pinpoint what you're aiming for, understanding the 'why' behind your goals is crucial... sound familiar? Are your goals driven by external pressures or comparison to others? Are you chasing someone else's idea of success?

In my journey, I've found that pursuing unrealistic ideals often stems from a lack of self-worth or confidence, or even as a means of self-sabotage, keeping me stuck in a victim mentality. Yes, I'm going there. Let me elaborate.

There have been times when I've set goals that were simply out of reach, driven by my longing to be seen as a leader or as a successful health coach. I believed that achieving these lofty standards would skyrocket my business and attract hordes of new clients. In this case, the story I believed was that I needed to shed 18% body fat to elevate my health to the next level, and only then would I attain true "happiness." If I fell short, well, I deemed myself a failure, unworthy of helping others.

The truth is, achieving the goal of dropping 18% body fat is technically possible. However, it would require a significant level of discipline and sacrifice over an extended period. Besides dealing with an autoimmune thyroid disease that directly impacts my metabolism, the journey would be quite challenging. Considering these factors alongside my true motivations, was pursuing this goal truly the best goal for me right now? Honestly, it wasn't. And even more importantly, the underlying reasons behind my desire to reduce body fat are fundamentally flawed.

What I now know to be true is that my ability to make a meaningful impact on people's lives through their health hinges on *my authenticity* and connecting with others right where they are and not my body fat percentage. Is reducing body fat a worthwhile endeavor? 100% yes. But setting a realistic goal, like reducing 5% body fat, and then breaking down the day-to-day actions I need to execute consistently will keep me empowered and out of a funk.

How do you know if you are in a funk?

- Are you always putting off getting active and telling yourself you'll start *someday*?
- Do you frequently tell yourself or others that you'll "start on Monday" or "after that event in 2 weeks"? When that Monday comes or the event is over, do you find another reason to delay your start?
- Are you frustrated with your progress and are getting discouraged in the journey?
- Does it appear as if everyone else pursuing similar goals has it easier than you do?

If the answer to any of these questions is "yes", then you are likely in a funk.

What does pursuing alignment look like?

Pursuing alignment starts with understanding where you stand on the spectrum between "it's too hard" and "chasing an unrealistic ideal." Often, when we view things as "too hard," we overcomplicate the process of getting started. On the other hand, striving for perfection or an unattainable ideal can leave us feeling overwhelmed and paralyzed. Recognizing where you fall on this spectrum allows you to focus on realistic, manageable steps that move you forward.

Your next best step:

If you find yourself in the "too hard" camp, the next best step is to ask yourself this question: *what can I do?* Even incorporating movement into your daily life is pretty doable. NEAT (non-exercise activity thermogenesis) activities like walking, gardening, taking the stairs, or even parking in the back of the lot will increase your movement.

Find a few friends who also want to be more active and start a walking group. Walking regularly offers numerous benefits, such as boosting energy, immune system, and creativity, while also lowering blood sugar, reducing the risk of cardiovascular disease, and easing joint pain.

If you find yourself chasing an unrealistic ideal, your next best step is to gain clarity on the real reason behind your goal. What is fueling your desire to achieve it? Taking the time to set a SMART goal (specific, measurable, achievable, relevant, and time-bound) can help ground your efforts and ensure they align with your values. This process requires a deeper level of awareness and honesty, but there's tremendous freedom on the other side of digging in.

When we pursue goals to boost our self-worth or keep up with others, we often set ourselves up for disappointment. By clarifying your true motivations, you can create goals that feel meaningful and achievable — keeping you aligned, fulfilled, and out of a funk.

Part 1 Alignment in Your Physical Health

Additional Resources to Take Your Next Best Step

To learn more about concepts like functional health, building healthy habits, incorporating movement and exercise, and rethinking your relationship with alcohol, visit the Part 1 Resources page. Explore tools, strategies, and additional insights to help you align your physical health with your goals and values.

Scan the QR code below to dive deeper or connect with Molly for personalized guidance.

Part 2:
Alignment in your mindset

In Part 2 we're diving into the world of mindset – the invisible force that shapes our outlook, influences how we show up, and, ultimately, determines how we experience life. It's easy to get stuck in a funk, but the good news is, we can shift our mindset and fundamentally change our lives.

Mindset isn't just a buzzword. It's the lens through which we see the world, and when that lens gets cloudy, it impacts *everything*. From our confidence and motivation to how we react to life's challenges. In this section, we'll break down the basics of mindset, understand how we get off track, and learn how to get back to basics with a Mindset Inventory™. This inventory will help us assess what we're consuming and build the awareness needed to make positive changes.

We'll start by adding specific, manageable changes to our routines – think morning habits, growth-oriented reading or listening, and changing our physical state. Simple tweaks that can spark big shifts. Then, we'll tackle the harder stuff – subtracting the things that no longer serve us. This might mean cutting out distractions or disrupting unhealthy habits. We'll start with the easy wins to build momentum, then move on to the trickier but necessary subtractions. Remember, change is challenging because our brains crave safety and familiarity, but together, we'll navigate this journey to a better mindset.

Chapter 5

The Power of the Mindset Inventory™

Our mindset is a collection of beliefs and attitudes that influence how we show up every day. Coming from a background in software and technology, I like to compare our brains to hardware and our mindset to software. Just like hardware runs on coded instructions to perform functions, our minds operate in a similar way. Sometimes, the software, or the source code we're operating from needs an upgrade.

Our mindset and outlook on life are shaped by a variety of sources. Experiences from our childhood and growing up play a significant role. The messages we received from parents, family members, friends, teachers, and coaches have all influenced us. These experiences, whether they met our emotional needs or overlooked them, become imprinted in our mindset as stories and beliefs we replay and live by.

Even more importantly, our current mindset is constantly being shaped by what we consume on a daily basis. This includes what we watch, read, and listen to, as well as the content we scroll through on our devices and the people we surround ourselves with.

One of the most overlooked aspects of maintaining a healthy mindset is how we spend our "whitespace time". Whitespace time refers to the unstructured moments in our day when we're not focused on specific tasks or obligations. It's those pockets of free time that allow for reflection, creativity, and mental relaxation. Unlike scheduled activities or work commitments, whitespace time is open-ended and flexible, giving us a chance to recharge, think freely, and explore new ideas without pressure. With the rise of social media platforms like Instagram, TikTok, Facebook, and YouTube, as well as the increasing divisiveness of traditional media, it's easy to lose hours of our day without even realizing it. This constant consumption can reinforce negative thinking and limiting beliefs, especially when we focus on content that highlights problems and conflicts or keeps us trapped in a cycle of comparison. Constant exposure to others "curated highlights" can lead to feelings of inadequacy, envy, and self-doubt, all of which fuel a negative mindset. We often don't realize that these seemingly benign activities profoundly influence how we show up in our daily lives.

Recognizing this influence was a turning point for me. During a period when I was feeling particularly stuck, I noticed how much time I was spending mindlessly scrolling through social media and binge-watching Netflix. These habits were contributing to my funk. So, I decided to make small changes, like cutting down on screen time and being more mindful about what I consumed. Almost immediately, I noticed an improvement in my mindset and outlook.

But here's the kicker: a few weeks later, I found myself sliding back into the same old funk. When I took a moment to reflect, I realized I had gradually gone back to my old habits because they were familiar and comfortable, like a default factory setting in my brain. Even though I knew these habits weren't serving me or what I wanted to create in my life, making a lasting change was going to require something more. This cycle of slipping back into a funk showed me the need for a more structured approach to keeping a healthy mindset.

That's when the Mindset Inventory™ was born. It's a simple, yet powerful tool that has been instrumental in helping me and many others stay out of the funk and show up as our best selves every day. It consists of several questions to assess whether someone might be out of alignment with what they are watching, reading, scrolling through, and listening to. Each time these questions are reviewed and consumption habits are assessed, it's likely to find some "whitespace time waster" that needs to be reined in. This process makes it easy to identify the areas that are dragging them down and allows for a conscious choice to shift, positioning them for a more positive mindset.

This inventory is built on a foundational principle: *what we consume shapes our thoughts, our thoughts mold our beliefs, our beliefs fuel our actions, and our actions dictate our results.* If we want to change our results, we need to start by assessing and changing our consumption habits. This is the beginning of a transformative journey toward a healthier, more positive mindset.

Here are some of the questions in the Mindset Inventory. Take a few minutes to answer them honestly and without judgment. Remember, the goal is simply to build your awareness.

- Outside of work, how often do you visit websites that inspire or motivate you?
- How often do you read or listen to books that help you grow personally or professionally?
- How much time do you spend scrolling social media or YouTube daily?
- How much time do you spend playing games on your phone daily?
- How much time do you spend playing video games daily?
- How often do you binge-watch TV shows or movies?
- How often do you feel your "whitespace" time is used productively?

- How often do you spend time with people who make you feel positive and uplifted?
- How often do you adhere to an established morning routine?

Each time I go through these questions, there's *always* one or two that stand out. They highlight where my recent actions have leaned too much into habits that keep me in a funk and feeling stuck.

How do you know if you are in a funk?

- Do you feel energized and excited about the day ahead, or do you feel tired, unmotivated, and dreading what's to come?
- Have you noticed a drop in your enthusiasm for activities that you used to enjoy?
- Are you withdrawing from friends and family, or feeling disconnected in your interactions with others?

What does pursuing alignment look like?

Pursuing alignment in this area begins with building your awareness muscle, especially around how you spend your "whitespace" or free time.

Take a moment to reflect on how you currently use your whitespace time. Are you engaging in activities that nourish your mind, body and soul, or are you falling into habits that leave you feeling drained and unfulfilled? Pursuing alignment means making conscious choices about how you fill these spaces in your day.

Your next best step:

Spend some time going through the Mindset Inventory to pinpoint where your consumption habits aren't serving you. If you don't like the results you're seeing in your life, it's time to go back to the basics—what you're consuming regularly—and make some changes.

Chapter 6

Empowering Your Mindset Through Addition

In the previous chapter, we dove into the Mindset Inventory™, a tool designed to help us become aware of the inputs shaping our mindset. By regularly taking stock of what we watch, read, scroll through, and listen to, we can identify which habits might be dragging us down. Awareness is the first step to change, but awareness alone isn't enough to pull us out of a funk. Let's dive in and start building the practices that will help us show up as our best selves every day.

One of the most powerful ways to curate a positive mindset is by gaining clarity on what we truly want. When our goals and desires are clear, we have a sense of direction and purpose that motivates us. It allows us to focus our energy on what truly matters, simplifying the process of deciding and taking actions that align with our values and aspirations.

To gain this clarity, start by taking some quiet time for yourself. This could be early in the morning before the hustle of the day begins, or in the evening when things have settled down. Use this time to reflect on what truly makes you happy and fulfilled. Ask yourself questions like, "What excites me?" "What activities or moments make me lose track of time?" "What values do I want to live by?"

Journaling can be a powerful tool in this process. Write down your thoughts, dreams, and aspirations without filtering yourself. Let it all out on paper. You might be surprised at what you uncover. Sometimes, the simple act of writing things down can bring a lot of clarity.

No matter how old you are, don't be afraid to dream big. Often, we limit ourselves by thinking small or believing that certain dreams are out of reach. Give yourself permission to envision a life that truly excites you. Once you have this clarity, it's time to support your new vision with positive influences. Incorporating uplifting content into your daily routine is a powerful and easy way to boost your mindset.

Feeding our minds with positive and growth-oriented material can shift our perspective and enhance our outlook. One of the best ways to do this is by reading and listening to books and podcasts on topics that interest you. For me, personal development podcasts have been a game-changer. They offer insights, advice, and stories that can ignite new ideas and keep me motivated. Whether it's learning about new habits, hearing success stories, or just getting a dose of positivity, the right podcasts can be like having an experienced mentor in your ear. I know I'm setting myself up for success when I'm regularly listening to the podcasts I subscribe to. When I'm in a funk, I'm usually behind on listening because I've prioritized binge-watching something I've seen before over keeping current with my favorite podcasts.

Another powerful source of inspiration is social media if it's managed intentionally. Social media is here to stay, and for the vast majority of us, it's a regular part of our lives. So, here's how to keep yourself out of a funk: curate your social media feeds to include content that encourages, inspires, and motivates you. Unfollow people or groups who promote divisiveness, conflict, or drama. We need to reduce the amount of negativity in our feeds and populate them with content that will add to our lives.

For instance, if you're passionate about health and wellness, follow experts in that field who share tips, recipes, and motivational content. If you love personal growth, seek out influencers and authors who provide insights and inspiration. The key is to surround yourself with content that fills your cup and lights you up.

Also, consider adding books, blogs, and articles to your daily routine. Dedicating even just 10-15 minutes a day to reading something uplifting or educational can help keep your mindset in a positive and growth-focused space.

It's not just about consuming content, though. Engage with it. Reflect on what you've learned, share it with others, and try to apply it in your own life. This active engagement helps to reinforce the positive messages and integrate them into your mindset.

By intentionally choosing content that inspires and educates, you're setting yourself up for a more positive and motivated mindset. These small, 1% additions of inspiration can accumulate, leading to big shifts in how you view the world and your place in it.

Next, let's talk about adding a morning routine to help curate a more positive mindset. Having a morning routine isn't just about starting the day doing the same actions; it's about taking control of our day rather than letting the day control us.

For me, starting the day with even just a few minutes of prayer, meditation, or mindfulness sets a powerful tone. It doesn't require much time, but the dividends it pays throughout the day are significant. It's a moment to center myself, set intentions for the day ahead, and reaffirm my worth *exactly as I am*. This mental preparation puts me in an empowered space to navigate whatever comes my way.

Equally important is creating space in our morning routine to identify and process our feelings and emotions, especially when facing big or challenging situations. Instead of burying or numbing these feelings, giving them room to be acknowledged and journaled about allows us to move through the day with clarity and purpose. By holding space for reflection and emotional processing each morning, we honor our emotional well-being and strengthen our resilience.

These practices are about adding positive elements to our lives that can transform our mindset. In the next chapter, we'll explore the equally important task of subtracting or reducing whitespace time wasters that keep us stuck.

How do you know if you are in a funk?

One clear sign you might be in a funk is falling back into consumption habits that aren't serving you. Are you spending too much time on social media or binge-watching TV? Have you neglected your personal growth activities like reading or listening to podcasts? These patterns can signal a need for more positive content, a consistent morning routine, or clarity about your desired outcomes.

What does pursuing alignment look like?

Pursuing alignment involves being aware when you slip into unhelpful patterns and strategically adding positive influences to your life. It's about recognizing the signs of a funk and making a conscious effort to include content and habits that uplift you. By building this awareness, you can actively choose activities and routines that support your well-being and keep you aligned with your goals.

Your next best step:

Consider what content aligns with your values and interests and make it a part of your routine. Start by identifying one positive addition, like listening to a motivational podcast or setting an inspiring morning routine. These small, intentional changes can significantly enhance your outlook and help you stay aligned with your goals.

Chapter 7

Clearing the Mindset Clutter by Subtracting

In the last chapter, we talked about the benefits of adding positive, personal development content into your daily routine. Now, it's time to discuss an even more powerful strategy: subtracting the distractions and habits that weigh down our mindset and outlook. Here's the deal: Adding more positive content is great, but it only gets you so far. Think of it as going from being stopped at a red light to moving at 20 miles per hour. It's a start, but it's not going to get you where you ultimately want to be.

Subtracting, while tougher, is like pressing the gas pedal to the floor. When you start removing or even just reducing those *excessive* distractions—like mindless social media scrolling, endless video gaming, consistently binge watching, and spending a lot of time with toxic people—it's like going from 20 mph to 80 mph. The real game changer? Doing both at the same time. Imagine the transformation when you not only add positive elements but also cut back on the activities and influences that drain your energy. Even a reduction in time spent on these activities can lead to a better mindset and help the positive additions gain more traction.

Here's the kicker—subtracting is freaking hard! It's uncomfortable, and it takes real effort. But trust me, it's worth it. We're going to dive deep into why subtracting or reducing time spent doing these activities is so powerful and how you can start making those tough but necessary changes.

For me, the challenge of subtracting became very real when a mentor, Doug Wood, asked me to identify one thing I could remove for 30 days that was consuming time I could be using to pursue my goals and create the life I wanted. Doug's premise was simple but powerful: in order to create space for what I said I wanted, I might need to "stop doing something" that's acting as a time suck.

When Doug first posed this challenge, I felt a pit in my stomach because I knew what that one thing was... remove the 5 streaming apps from my phone. After I stopped drinking alcohol earlier that year, the way I would "unwind" at the end of the workday was to pop open one of the streaming apps on my phone and binge-watch episodes of shows I'd seen multiple times. It was my way of checking out and escaping the day's stresses. Invariably, one episode would lead to two or three and I'd end up disengaged from my family and not pursuing *what I said I wanted*.

So, I took Doug's challenge to heart and removed all those apps from my phone for 30 days. Interestingly, after I removed the streaming apps, I experienced a strong sense of cognitive dissonance. Suddenly, I had a lot more time, but I felt lost and unsure how to use it effectively. The idea of diving into the work needed to achieve my goals didn't seem appealing, and I often felt unmotivated. This internal conflict—between my intention to build my business and my resistance to taking action—created significant mental discomfort.

It was like a tug-of-war between wanting to move forward and the inertia of old habits. But here's the key: This cognitive dissonance is a sign that the shift is happening. Once I pushed through that initial discomfort and started engaging in the work or finding new, productive ways to spend my time, the mindset shift began to occur. The addition of new, positive habits eventually filled the void left by the subtractions, and the discomfort faded as the new routines started to take hold. This cycle of subtracting, feeling dissonance, and eventually finding clarity has become a crucial and predictable part of this process.

When you subtract one thing from your routine, it's important to be aware of what you might be replacing it with. Sometimes, without even realizing it, we fill that gap with something that doesn't actually help us create a more positive mindset.

Take my own experience, for example. When I decided to stop drinking alcohol, I had to figure out what to do with that time at the end of my workday. So, I started binge-watching TV shows on my phone and playing Farm Heroes Saga. It felt like a way to unwind, but it wasn't really serving me. When I finally removed the streaming apps from my phone, I just moved the binge-watching to the TV while still playing those games. And when I took the games off my phone, I found myself needing something else to fill that time. That's when I realized the pattern: every time I removed something, I just replaced it with something else—often something that wasn't truly helping me.

I knew I needed to find a healthier, more productive way to transition from my workday, something that wouldn't work against me. That's when I decided to hire my meditation coach, Deanna Wheeler. Together, we built a custom playlist of meditations specifically designed to help me transition during that critical time of day. Incorporating meditation into my routine has been life changing. It's helped me stay present, aligned, and in tune with what I'm feeling and thinking. Instead of filling the void with distractions, I'm now using that time to attune and reconnect with myself, and it's made all the difference.

There are times when you may not be able to completely eliminate or subtract certain habits or activities from your life. They might be necessary, or they may serve a specific purpose that aligns with your goals. In these cases, it's all about how you manage and engage with them.

Take social media, for instance. While eliminating it entirely isn't realistic for many of us—especially when it's a key way we connect with others—it's essential to be intentional about how we use it. When I'm on social media to post, connect, and genuinely engage in conversations, that's purposeful and aligned with my goals. But when I start mindlessly scrolling through reels for 30 minutes (or more, let's be honest), it's a *different story*. Before I know it, I'm lost in a rabbit hole of other people's highlight reels, comparing my life to their perfectly curated content. Not only does this drain my time, but it also pulls me into a cycle of comparison and self-doubt.

So, what's the solution? It's simple, but it's worked for me: set a timer. When the timer goes off, it's my cue to *physically* move my body—get up, water the plants, make dinner or anything else that gets me moving. This small shift changes your state and signals your mind that it's time to transition to the next task. It's a practical way to ensure that your time on social media remains purposeful and doesn't derail the momentum you're building towards a more positive mindset.

How do you know if you are in a funk?

It often shows up when you've made some progress, but instead of feeling proud or accomplished, you're stuck in a state of frustration. You might be asking yourself, "Why isn't this enough?" or "Why am I not further along?" Even though you're moving forward, something feels off, and you're not experiencing the momentum or joy you expected. It's that nagging sense that, despite your efforts, you're not where you want to be—and it leaves you feeling stuck and dissatisfied.

What does pursuing alignment look like?

Pursuing alignment is about more than just making changes; it's about consistently checking in to see if those changes are working for you. Building your self-awareness muscle means asking yourself, "Are the subtractions I've made actually improving my mindset and outlook? Do I feel more aligned and at peace, or am I still struggling with old patterns?" This isn't a one-time process but an ongoing practice of ensuring that the steps you're taking are genuinely setting you up for success and a more positive mindset.

Your next best step:

If you've subtracted or reduced some things but are still feeling stuck, it's time to revisit your Mindset Inventory™. Take a fresh look at what might still be out of whack. Consider where you're spending most of your whitespace time—what activities or habits might be contributing to that feeling of being stuck? Once you identify the area that's still out of alignment, make a conscious decision to further reduce or eliminate it. This intentional adjustment helps you move closer to a more balanced and positive mindset.

Part 2 Alignment in Your Mindset

Additional Resources to Take Your Next Best Step

Want to go deeper into the **Mindset Inventory**™, overcoming limiting beliefs, building emotional resilience, and aligning your mindset with your goals? Visit the Part 2 page for actionable strategies and insights to empower your thinking and create a healthier mindset.

Scan the QR code below

to access more resources for additional support.

Part 3:
Alignment in your purpose

I believe we are here at this specific time in the world on purpose and for a purpose. Each of our life's experiences—whether they've lifted us up or knocked us down—has the potential to bring us closer to that purpose. But let's be honest: our purpose can sometimes feel elusive, like a distant vision we just can't seem to grasp. It's easy for our purpose to get clouded by the stories we tell ourselves about our experiences, often leaving us feeling stuck or unsure of the path ahead.

Ed Mylett fiercely says, "You were born to do something great with your life." And I believe that to my core. But how do we figure out what that "something impactful" is? How do we know if we're on the right track or if we've veered off course?

Through my own journey, I've come to realize that finding alignment in our purpose isn't about a single moment of clarity or a grand revelation. It's about consistently using your unique skills and talents, engaging in activities that bring you true enjoyment, and placing yourself in an environment that allows you to thrive. I've combined these elements into what I call the **STEP Formula**™, where **Skills + True Enjoyment + Environment = Purpose Alignment**.

In the chapters that follow, we'll dive into the STEP Formula and how it can help you realign with your purpose. You'll learn how to uncover and leverage your unique Skills/Talents, identify and prioritize what brings you True Enjoyment, and create an Environment that supports your growth and fulfillment.

If you're in a funk with your purpose, it's a signal that something needs adjusting. While it's normal to feel stuck or question your path, the STEP Formula offers clarity and practical tools to help you move through those challenges and realign with what truly matters to you.

By the end of these chapters, you'll not only understand how to use the STEP Formula effectively but also feel empowered to recognize misalignments and take meaningful steps toward a life of greater energy and fulfillment.

Chapter 8

Unlocking the Strength of Your Skills

We all have skills and talents that are unique to us. These innate abilities are part of who we are, and over the course of our lives, we've honed them, adding layers of skills that shape how we navigate the world. Some people are naturally wired to be process-driven, seeing a clear order in which tasks need to be completed. They thrive on structure, the satisfaction of checking off boxes, and knowing exactly what steps to take next. For them, a well-organized plan is like a roadmap, guiding them from point A to point B with confidence and clarity. They find comfort in routine and predictability, allowing them to maintain focus and momentum as they work toward their goals.

On the other hand, some people are big-picture thinkers, the visionaries who can see the grand plan from a bird's-eye view. They are inspired by the possibilities, driven by ideas, and fueled by the potential they see on the horizon. Details might feel cumbersome or secondary to them because their minds are constantly weaving together the broader vision. They are the dreamers, the innovators who push boundaries and imagine what could be, often leaving the finer points to be figured out along the way.

Our natural inclinations aren't flaws—they're reflections of our unique wiring. Each of us has a "bent," a way of approaching the world that's deeply rooted in our personality, and it often traces back to childhood. These tendencies are not just random quirks; they are powerful indicators of the skills and talents that set us apart.

Think back to when you were a kid: were you the one who naturally took charge, organizing the games and making sure everyone had a role? Or were you the creative mastermind, always coming up with new ideas and imagining different scenarios for everyone to play out? Maybe you were the quiet observer, carefully noticing details others missed, or the peacekeeper, always finding ways to bring people together. These early behaviors are more than just childhood memories—they're clues to your core strengths and how you're naturally wired to operate.

As we grow, these tendencies often evolve, but they remain at the heart of how we interact with the world. The organizer might find themselves excelling in project management or leadership roles, where their ability to structure and direct is invaluable. The creative thinker might thrive in environments that allow for innovation and out-of-the-box solutions. The observer might become a skilled analyst, deeply understanding patterns that others overlook. And the peacekeeper might excel in roles requiring diplomacy, empathy, and conflict resolution.

Recognizing and leveraging these intrinsic traits isn't just about navigating life's challenges with greater ease—it's a crucial step on the path to finding your aligned purpose. By embracing how you're uniquely designed, you set the stage for deeper fulfillment and success in your journey.

So now, it's time to roll up our sleeves and gain some clarity around what those skills and talents are. To do that, let's start by asking a few key questions that can help you uncover and label these abilities:

- What is something you do that you feel you're good at?
- What comes easy to you, almost like second nature?
- What gives you a burst of energy when you're doing it?
- Conversely, what tasks tend to drain your energy?

- What have others recognized in you as a skill or talent?
- When have you felt most proud of your work or achievements?
- What types of activities do you find yourself naturally gravitating toward?

Reflecting on these questions will help you uncover the skills and talents that are uniquely yours, allowing you to recognize and leverage them in alignment with your purpose.

To illustrate how these questions can reveal your skills and talents, let me share a personal example. When I was 7 or 8 years old, I vividly remember my mom saying, "Molly, you are such a good cleaner!" Apparently, I had tackled a cleaning or organizing task with surprising efficiency—though I can't recall exactly what it was. What I do remember is the impact of her words. Decades later, I can still hear her voice affirming something I did well. This early feedback has stuck with me and highlighted a skill that was evident from a young age.

Recognizing your skills and talents is more than just knowing what you're good at—it's about understanding how those strengths align with the roles and tasks you take on in life. When you're in sync with your natural abilities, work can feel fulfilling and energizing. But when there's a disconnect, it can lead to frustration, unhappiness, and a sense of being stuck.

I remember the moment I realized just how misaligned my corporate role had become. As my responsibilities evolved, I felt myself drifting further away from what I was truly good at. Each passing day, the gap between my skills and the demands of the role grew wider, but it wasn't until March of 2023 that I finally had the courage to voice it. During a conversation with my boss, I said what felt like the scariest sentence of my adult life:

"If success in this role is going to require me to spend 50% or more of my time talking to large foundations and national nonprofits, then I don't think I'm the right person for this role."

Saying those words was terrifying. I had to muster all my strength just to keep my composure, because what I was really saying was, "I don't fit here anymore."

Despite holding a C-level position for three years, I had found myself in a career funk. I'm someone who loves to roll up my sleeves, get things done, and lead teams to success. But as the role shifted, I felt myself moving further away from my core strengths. For 25+ years, my career has been centered around software and technology operations—not nonprofit business development. And as much as I tried to force myself to adapt, I couldn't shake the feeling that I was in the wrong lane.

The conversations about cultivating new partnerships in the nonprofit sector became more frequent, and with each discussion, my imposter syndrome grew. I spent months feeling inadequate, trying to fill a gap that wasn't mine to fill. The more I forced myself to adapt, the more I felt like I was failing—not just at the job, but at being the leader I thought I was supposed to be.

In an attempt to regain control, I focused on the areas where I knew I excelled: operations management, process optimization, and team development. Those were my sweet spots—the places where I knew I could add value. But the growing demands of nonprofit business development loomed large, and every time I had to step into that world, the feelings of inadequacy would rush back in.

I coped the best way I knew how: with a daily glass (or three) of wine after work, zoning out in front of shows I'd already seen a hundred times. It was my escape—a way to numb the feelings of being out of place in a career I had worked so hard to build. I knew it wasn't healthy. My sleep was terrible, and I woke up every morning feeling irritable and run down.

But I kept pushing. I kept trying to force my "round" skills into a "square" role. It wasn't sustainable. I was drained, exhausted, and scared. I knew, deep down, that I was in the wrong lane. But I also feared what it would mean if I admitted it—if I admitted that I wasn't the right fit for this role. What would people think? Would I be seen as a failure? I told myself all kinds of stories about not being enough, about letting down the other women in the company who looked up to me.

And then, that pivotal conversation with my boss happened. It was terrifying, but it was also liberating. In that moment, I was finally acknowledging the truth my gut had been telling me all along: I wasn't the best person for this role, and that was okay. After that conversation, something unexpected happened: an open dialogue.

My boss didn't react with judgment or frustration—instead, we started discussing how we could reshape my role to align better with my strengths. The nonprofit business development responsibilities that had been weighing me down? Those could go to someone else on the team, someone with more experience in that area. It wasn't about me failing; it was about recognizing where I added the most value. They'd backfill my role with someone who had the nonprofit expertise, and I could get back to what I was good at—operations, process optimization, team development. It was like a weight had been lifted.

For the first time in months, I felt like I could breathe. I could finally step into the areas where I excelled and continue to contribute to a company I genuinely loved working for. And the best part? This shift opened up more space in my life—more bandwidth to focus on something that had been on my heart for years: building my coaching business.

By letting go of what wasn't working and leaning into my skills and talent - and more importantly *what fueled me*, I was getting out of the funk. I wasn't just surviving—I was finally stepping fully into who I was meant to be. Identifying my core skills and talents and seeing how they could serve the company brought an overwhelming sense of relief. The weight of living daily in imposter syndrome and low self-worth began to lift. Instead of forcing myself into a role that didn't fit, I could operate in my "lane" where I thrived. For the first time in a long while, I felt like I was contributing in a way that aligned with my strengths, and that lifted the pressure of misalignment. The clarity and confidence that came with living in alignment not only improved my performance but also restored my confidence.

Identifying your skills and talents isn't just a nice-to-have—it's the foundation for a fulfilled and aligned life. When you're stuck in a role that doesn't play to your strengths, frustration and that "stuck" feeling can take over, eventually landing you in a funk. Recognizing what you're naturally good at is the key to finding purpose, satisfaction, and fulfillment both at work and beyond.

How do you know if you are in a funk?

You might feel stuck, like you're just going through the motions, or even question your purpose in the roles you currently occupy. It's not always an all-consuming feeling; sometimes, it's that quiet voice that whispers, "Is this it?" You might notice that the tasks and activities that once energized you now feel like a burden. Perhaps you're irritable, more tired than usual, or find yourself avoiding responsibilities because they feel overwhelming. This feeling of being out of alignment can manifest in different ways: a lack of motivation, trouble focusing, or even a dull, persistent feeling of unhappiness. If you're constantly daydreaming about being somewhere else or doing something different, it's a strong indicator that you're in a funk.

What does pursuing alignment look like?

It's a process of peeling back the layers to rediscover what lights you up and energizes you. When you're pursuing alignment, you start to make choices that bring your life back into harmony with your strengths and passions. This could mean making small adjustments—like carving out time for activities that bring you joy—or it might involve bigger changes, like shifting roles at work or even changing careers. The key is to move towards tasks and roles that feel natural and fulfilling, where you can truly shine. You'll know you're on the right path when you start to feel more energized, focused, and engaged in your daily life. The things that once felt like a burden start to feel more manageable, and you find yourself more present and satisfied in your everyday tasks.

Your next best step:

Start by revisiting the questions we explored earlier in this chapter—reflect on what you're naturally good at and where your passions lie. Then, look at your current situation: Where is the misalignment happening? Is it in your job, your daily routines, or perhaps even in your relationships? Once you've pinpointed the area of disconnection, begin to brainstorm ways to bridge that gap. This might involve setting new goals, seeking out opportunities that better align with your strengths, or even having a candid conversation with someone who can support you in making these changes. Remember, this is a process—it doesn't have to happen overnight. But by taking one intentional step at a time, you'll gradually move out of the funk and into a space where you feel more aligned, fulfilled, and in tune with your true self.

Chapter 9

Tapping into What You Truly Enjoy

In the first part of our formula to find alignment in our purpose, we focused on identifying what we're good at—our skills and talents. But being good at something is just the beginning. The next step is to assess whether it's something you *actually enjoy doing*. This is where you build on the foundation of your abilities by ensuring that what you do also brings you genuine fulfillment and joy.

So, what does it *feel* like to do what you enjoy? Joy isn't just a fleeting moment of happiness; it's a deep, lasting sense of contentment that comes from engaging in activities that resonate with your true self. It's that feeling of alignment when you're doing something that not only uses your talents but also fills you up rather than drains you.

When you're engaged in activities that align with your skills that also bring you genuine joy, you often find yourself operating in a state of "flow." This is when you're so fully immersed in what you're doing that time seems to disappear, and you're completely absorbed in the task at hand. Achieving flow can enhance your performance, increase your creativity, and deepen your satisfaction because you're doing something that resonates deeply with your core.

But joy doesn't just stop at feeling good in the moment. It also drives personal fulfillment. When you're doing what you enjoy, you're aligning your daily activities with your true self. This intrinsic fulfillment comes from knowing that you're not just going through the motions but actively engaging in something that has meaning and value for you. This alignment helps you move away from seeking external validation and instead, find contentment from within.

Following my conversation with my boss in March 2023, we worked together to reshape my role to better align with my strengths and passions. This transition was both empowering and intimidating. It forced me to confront long-held beliefs about success, my self-image, and how others might view this shift. Having climbed the corporate ladder for nearly 15 years as the only female executive, I felt the pressure of my title and the growing responsibilities that were drifting away from my core competencies, leaving me unhappy and disconnected.

The revised role allowed me to focus on operational aspects where I truly excelled and offloaded responsibilities that were outside my skill set. It felt like I had finally found my lane on a six-lane highway. Before the change, I was struggling in the wrong lane—overwhelmed by tasks that didn't align with my strengths.

Once I was in my lane, everything shifted. I experienced a surge of energy and creativity, as if I had seamlessly aligned with the work that truly suited me. With the weight of a partially misaligned role lifted, I could fully embrace and enhance my strengths. This shift allowed me to excel even more in what I do best, bringing greater enjoyment and a renewed sense of purpose to my work.

Being in the right lane meant I could focus entirely on my core skills without the burden of misalignment. The result was a more satisfying and productive experience, where I felt fully engaged and capable in my role. This shift wasn't just a change in responsibilities; it was a profound realignment that reignited my passion for my work. I had a deep knowing in my gut that I was in the best position to make the most significant impact, and that realization filled me with a profound sense of purpose and satisfaction. I was doing what I enjoyed.

Yet, even when you're doing something you love, challenges and obstacles are an inevitable part of the journey. These difficulties push you to refine your skills, think creatively, and adapt to new situations. Rather than detracting from your satisfaction, they become opportunities to deepen your expertise and strengthen your commitment to your work. Facing and overcoming these challenges enhances your abilities, builds confidence, and offers valuable insights that ultimately improve your performance and growth.

This process not only makes you better at what you enjoy but also enriches your sense of fulfillment. Overcoming challenges reinforces your dedication and makes the experience of doing what you love even more rewarding. The satisfaction of mastering a difficult task or navigating a problem adds to the joy and sense of accomplishment you derive from your passion. Each obstacle you overcome strengthens your skills and deepens your appreciation for what you do, making the pursuit of your passions even more meaningful and satisfying.

Yet, even as you excel and find joy in overcoming challenges, it's crucial to differentiate between being good at something and genuinely enjoying it. For instance, remember when my mom told me I was a "good cleaner" when I was young? Sure, I had the skill, but I don't enjoy cleaning. This highlights an essential truth: having the talent for something doesn't necessarily mean you'll *enjoy doing it.* Listening to your gut is vital when determining whether you truly enjoy an activity, regardless of your skill level.

There are a few key signs that might indicate you're not truly enjoying what you're doing. For instance, if you're consistently lacking enthusiasm for tasks that once excited you, it's a good sign something might be off. When we genuinely enjoy what we're doing, it usually lights us up and makes us eager to dive in, rather than feeling like a never-ending chore.

Another important indicator is if you're feeling a lot of frustration or irritation. While occasional bumps in the road are normal, if you're constantly feeling exasperated, it's worth paying attention to. Similarly, if you're left feeling drained or depleted after working on something, it's a signal that it might not be the right fit. Activities that bring us joy generally leave us feeling refreshed and fulfilled.

Procrastination is also a telltale sign. If you find yourself constantly making excuses or putting off tasks you're skilled at, it might be time to reassess. When we're truly passionate about something, we're more likely to jump into it with enthusiasm rather than finding reasons to avoid it. Also, consider whether these tasks align with your sense of purpose and values. If there's a disconnect, it could mean you're not quite where you're meant to be.

If you're noticing these signs, it's important to give yourself permission to explore what genuinely brings you joy and satisfaction. Your journey to fulfillment is all about finding and embracing what truly resonates with you, not just sticking with something because you're good at it.

It's important to remember that others might be surprised or even confused when they learn that you don't enjoy something you're naturally skilled at. They might not understand why you're not passionate about what seems like an obvious fit for you. But here's the deal: their opinions don't dictate your path to fulfillment. True alignment in your purpose comes from you recognizing what you're good at and what genuinely excites you. You'll know when you're in the right place because it will resonate deeply with you, regardless of what others think.

Often, the opinions of others are shaped by their own desires or shortcomings. Their surprise or disapproval may stem from something they wish they had or a lack they feel in their own lives. Ultimately, finding what truly brings you joy and satisfaction is a personal journey. It's about embracing what feels right for you, not adhering to someone else's expectations or perceptions.

How do you know if you are in a funk?

Do you find you're consistently procrastinating, feeling frustrated, or experiencing irritation? If these feelings are persistent and not just temporary responses to challenges that can occur even when you're engaged in activities you love, it's a sign that your level of enjoyment is lacking. When you're in a funk, these negative feelings tend to be a constant presence rather than occasional bumps in the road.

What does pursuing alignment look like?

Pursuing alignment is a process of discovering and integrating what genuinely energizes and fulfills you. This involves identifying activities that bring you joy and satisfaction and finding ways to weave them into your life. It's about building momentum by gradually incorporating these elements, which can initially feel overwhelming. The journey involves recognizing what truly excites you and making space for it, whether through your current work or personal pursuits. As you begin this process, you'll start to see shifts in how you engage with your daily activities, leading to a more fulfilling and aligned life.

Your next best step:

Start by identifying what you enjoy and don't enjoy doing and reflect on why. This clarity will help you understand your preferences and provide insight into how you can better align your activities with your passions. Gaining this understanding not only fuels your motivation but also guides you in making more informed decisions about where to focus your energy moving forward.

Chapter 10

The Impact of the Right Environment

In this chapter, we'll dive into the final piece of the alignment in your purpose formula: being in the right environment for using your skills and talents in ways you enjoy. This isn't just about corporate culture— whether you're balancing a traditional career, diving into a side hustle, volunteering, or involved in any other kind of organization, the environment where you apply your skills and passions truly makes all the difference.

You might be deeply skilled and genuinely passionate about what you do, but if you're doing it in an environment that doesn't align with your values or fails to recognize your contributions, your satisfaction can quickly fade. An ideal environment not only supports your talents but also creates a space where you feel seen, heard, and valued for what you bring to the table. It's about more than just the work you do—it's about being in an environment that fosters collaboration, respect, and appreciation. The practices, atmosphere, and the way people engage with each other can significantly impact how effective and fulfilled you feel while using your skills.

The environment you choose to work in can either elevate or drain your passion and energy. I've seen this firsthand in my own career. In over 25 years of experience in the business world, I've learned that people thrive in environments where they are celebrated rather than just tolerated. Time is our most valuable resource, and where we choose to spend it has a profound impact on how we show up in our lives. When we're in settings where our contributions are genuinely recognized and appreciated, we become more invested in what we're doing. When we feel truly valued, it boosts our engagement and enthusiasm, making our work experience not only more fulfilling but also more productive.

My husband, Geoff, once worked for a company where the environment was toxic from day one. The culture operated like a tournament—everyone was in competition with each other, and survival meant working against your peers, not alongside them. Knowledge was hoarded as power, and only those with access to senior leadership could position themselves as indispensable. If you weren't part of the inner circle or didn't have someone from that circle vouching for you, you were treated as disposable. Favor wasn't earned through hard work or collaboration but by making the right people look good.

From early on, Geoff was thrown into high-stakes situations. He was often given little notice before being asked to join meetings where he had to provide detailed information on the spot. Despite his consistent accuracy and thoroughness—even when delivering hard-to-swallow truths—he always felt on edge, wondering if he was being set up to take the blame for something outside of his control. This constant uncertainty and tension created a persistent funk, making him feel as if every move could backfire and that he was trapped in a never-ending cycle of stress and fear.

The impact on Geoff's well-being was profound. Mentally and emotionally, the toxic environment chipped away at his confidence and sense of self-worth. He couldn't fully relax, even at home. His mind was constantly racing, replaying conversations, second-guessing decisions, and trying to stay one step ahead of potential fallout. Stress levels soared, leading to physical symptoms like high blood pressure and a constant state of fight-or-flight. He was most certainly in a funk.

You might wonder, "Why did he stay in this job?" It's a valid question. For a long time, Geoff believed he could work hard enough to earn favor and rise above the cutthroat, zero-sum game culture. He thought that if he just pushed through, things would eventually get better. But the reality was more complicated. During a major economic downturn, the pressure of providing for our family weighed heavily on him. The toxic environment had drained him mentally and emotionally, making the idea of starting fresh and facing interviews feel like an insurmountable challenge. He was so depleted that he struggled to believe there could be a better opportunity out there. Survival mode had taken over.

When Geoff finally left the company, it was like a huge weight had been lifted off his shoulders. He immediately felt a sense of relief that allowed him to gain some much-needed perspective. Only then did he fully realize how toxic the environment had been and how deeply it had affected him. He understood that no matter how skilled or passionate he was, being in an environment that didn't foster collaboration, growth, or mutual respect would never be sustainable.

Geoff's story is a powerful example of how even if you're in a role where you're using your skills and talents and doing work you enjoy, the wrong environment can still put you in a funk. When the environment doesn't align with your values or support your personal and professional growth, it can leave you feeling drained and miserable. The ideal environment is more than just a place to work—it's a space that allows you to thrive, feel valued, and contribute meaningfully.

Now, you might be thinking, *"How does this apply if I own my own business?"* Whether you're running a large company or a solo operation, creating an ideal environment is just as important. Even as a business owner, it's crucial to spend time in spaces where you feel seen, heard, and valued—and that's not always easy to do when you're the one at the helm. From my own experience building a coaching business, I've learned that being intentional about the environments you choose is everything. If you're not already in a space that fosters growth, learning, and collaboration, you've got two options: find a room where you can plug in, or create the room yourself and invite others.

I've done both, and it's made all the difference in how I show up in my life, my business, and even in my corporate role. Sometimes that means joining virtual groups or attending conferences where I can connect with like-minded people who challenge me to grow. Other times, it's about creating a community of my own—whether that's a mastermind, a coaching circle, or even just a regular meet-up with peers. These environments allow me to learn, collaborate, and feel truly supported, which, in turn, helps me show up better for my clients, my family, and my work.

When I started my health coaching business over five years ago, I had no idea how much my environment would shape my journey. I joined a community of other health coaches who were all on the same mission—holding each other accountable in our health while helping others create long-term, sustainable changes in their lives. What I found in that group was unlike anything I'd ever experienced before.

This wasn't just a "business group" where people looked out for themselves. Every single person I met, right up to the founder and president of the company, genuinely wanted to see everyone win. Whether it was about growing our businesses or staying on track with our own health goals, there was this incredible energy of support and accountability. It felt like being part of something bigger, where personal growth and living with integrity were just as important as the work we were doing.

Week after week, I've been poured into—challenged (in the best way) to face my fears and go after the life I truly want. Because of this environment, I've grown personally and professionally more than I ever thought possible. It's shaped not only how I show up for my clients but also how I show up in all areas of my life. The growth I've experienced in the last five years is second to none, and it all started with being part of a community that truly sees, hears, and pushes me to be my best.

When it comes to finding an ideal environment for growth, sometimes the best spaces are those that push you just outside your comfort zone. A couple of years ago, I joined a networking group that embodied this principle perfectly. This wasn't just any networking group—it was intentionally crafted to drive real transformation in both personal and professional realms. Through it, I gained access to top-tier guest speakers—business leaders and industry experts—and had the opportunity to engage deeply, connect authentically, and learn from individuals making significant impacts in their fields.

I'll be honest—this "room" challenges me in ways that can be uncomfortable. The people in this group are accomplishing remarkable things, and there are moments when I question whether I truly belong. But that's exactly why it has been the ideal environment for me. Being in a space that keeps me on the edge has stretched me in unexpected ways. It's not always easy, but this discomfort has encouraged me to dream bigger and believe in new possibilities for myself.

When you're doing something new and pushing boundaries, encountering a funk is almost inevitable. The discomfort, self-doubt, and frustration that come with stepping into unfamiliar territory are part of the process. However, being surrounded by people who genuinely want to see you succeed—who foster authenticity and challenge you to keep moving forward—makes all the difference. This environment, whether virtual or in person, demonstrates that the right space can be crucial in overcoming a funk and building momentum. It's about finding a place where you're constantly being challenged, lifted up, and encouraged to see beyond your limitations. That's how you break free from stagnation and start making meaningful progress.

How do you know if you are in a funk?

You might be in a funk if you consistently feel unseen, unheard, or undervalued in your environment, particularly if there's a lack of collaboration, teamwork, or alignment with the organization's goals. If you're a business owner and find yourself feeling isolated, drained, or uninspired, it's a strong sign that your environment may not be supporting your well-being or growth. The absence of a collaborative spirit and alignment with the mission can lead to stagnation and frustration. Recognizing these signs is crucial for identifying whether it's time to seek a more supportive and engaging space that fosters growth and connection.

What does pursuing alignment look like?

Pursuing alignment often requires the courage to step back and gain perspective on your environment, especially when it's draining your energy and enthusiasm, much like Geoff experienced. It's easy to stay stuck in familiar situations because they offer a sense of comfort, even if they're not ideal. Acknowledging that your environment might be contributing to your struggles takes real bravery. It involves evaluating whether the space you're in supports your growth and aligns with your values. Sometimes, recognizing that the environment is actively sucking the life out of you is the first step toward making meaningful changes. It's about having the courage to confront the reality of your surroundings and deciding to seek out or create a space that truly fosters your well-being and development.

Your next best step:

If you recognize that you're not in an ideal environment, it's likely you're operating from an empty cup every day. To shift this, your next best step is to connect with a group or community that is encouraging and motivating, where you genuinely feel seen, heard, and valued. Surround yourself with people who uplift you and provide the support and affirmation you need. By getting your cup filled in this life-affirming environment, you'll be better equipped to contribute positively and help others fill their cups as well. Once you've experienced the boost from being in a nurturing space, you can then look to make more substantial changes to the other environments in your life, ensuring they also align with your growth and well-being.

Chapter 11

Working the STEP™ Formula

In the past few chapters, we've explored the **STEP** Formula for finding alignment in your purpose: **Skills + True Enjoyment + Environment = Purpose Alignment**. Each component is vital, but the real magic happens when all three come together. It's when these elements align that we experience true fulfillment and purpose.

But let's be real—many of us find ourselves in a funk because one or more parts of this formula are missing, especially in our work lives. Maybe you're using your skills at your job but aren't in an environment that supports your growth, or perhaps you're in a great culture but not doing work you truly enjoy. It's easy to get stuck when things feel out of sync, and that's when the funk creeps in.

Here's the good news: you don't have to have all three parts of the STEP Formula in the work that pays the bills. The key is finding an outlet where you can apply your Skills and talents, experience True Enjoyment, and be in an ideal Environment, whether it's through a hobby, volunteer work, or a side hustle. When you find a place where you can truly align with the STEP Formula, you'll start to lift out of the funk—even if it's not happening in your 9-to-5.

We often fall into the trap of thinking our job has to be the sole source of our fulfillment. When it doesn't deliver, it can feel like a heavy weight of misalignment. Understanding that fulfillment can flow from various areas of your life helps ease the pressure to "have it all" at work.

You might still feel a bit out of sync in one area but having an outlet where you can truly engage with your purpose can bring fulfillment. This chapter is about putting it all together so you can see the bigger picture and take your next best step toward alignment.

Because we spend so much time in jobs that provide our primary income, I'll walk you through a few scenarios of the STEP formula— where parts of it might be present or missing, and what you can do about it. But remember this: It's entirely possible, and often beneficial, to find alignment through multiple outlets, like a side hustle, volunteering, or participating in groups that resonate with you. The ultimate goal? To have all parts of the STEP formula working in harmony, not just in your main job but across various areas of your life.

When Skills Are Missing, But True Enjoyment and Environment Are Present

This was the case in my own story. While there were aspects of my role where I thrived because I enjoyed the work and was in a positive environment, one significant part of my job was misaligned with my skills.

I found myself grappling with imposter syndrome, struggling with mental and emotional stress because I lacked the necessary skills for that particular aspect of the role. Despite my efforts to work harder and overcome these gaps, the mismatch was a constant source of frustration and self-doubt.

Fortunately, I was able to collaborate with my company to adjust my role so that I could concentrate on the areas where my skills were strong. By shifting my responsibilities to fit my strengths, I was able to reduce the distress and start operating from a place of confidence and aligned purpose.

If you're in a similar situation where you enjoy your work and are in a great environment but find that your skills aren't fully aligned with all aspects of your role, it's crucial to address this misalignment. Whether it's seeking additional training, adjusting your responsibilities, or finding a different role that better fits your skill set, taking steps to close this gap can significantly impact your sense of purpose and fulfillment.

When Skills and Environment Are Present, But True Enjoyment Is Missing

This situation can be challenging because, while you're in a great environment and using your skills, the lack of enjoyment can still lead to purpose misalignment.

If you find yourself in this position, it's worth exploring whether there are projects or initiatives within your company that align with your interests and passions. This might mean taking on additional work outside your core responsibilities, but if it sparks joy and fulfillment, it's a worthwhile effort. Look for opportunities where you can apply your skills in ways that might be more engaging and enjoyable.

Additionally, keep an eye out for other roles or positions within the company that offer work you find more captivating. Since you're already in a positive environment and your skills are valued, it might be a matter of finding the "right seat on the bus." By seeking out projects or roles that align with your interests, you can shift your experience from one of dissatisfaction to one of genuine fulfillment.

In essence, even if your core responsibilities aren't currently sparking joy, engaging in additional work that resonates with your passions can help you find greater purpose and satisfaction within the same supportive environment.

When Skills and True Enjoyment Are Present, But the Environment Isn't Great

This was Geoff's story—he was using his skills and talents, enjoying the actual work, but the toxic environment overshadowed everything else.

To address this, seek out advice from trusted colleagues or mentors who can offer constructive support without falling into gossip. Establishing healthy boundaries is also essential; make sure you protect your personal time and energy from the negative impact of the work environment. Engaging in positive initiatives, like joining employee resource groups (ERGs) or participating in corporate social responsibility (CSR) activities, can also help improve your experience.

Ultimately, you need to assess whether this company aligns with your long-term goals and values. If it doesn't, it might be time to consider if this is the right place for you in the long run.

By taking these steps, you can work on improving your experience and find more alignment with your purpose, even if the environment isn't ideal.

When 2 or More Parts of the Formula Are Missing - Now What?

If you find yourself in a situation where two or more parts of the purpose formula are missing, it's essential to take a step back and evaluate why you're staying in your current role. Ask yourself if the reasons for staying truly justify the feelings of misalignment you're experiencing. Is it worth spending every day feeling out of alignment? Misalignment doesn't just affect your work—it trickles down and impacts other areas of your life as well.

From my own experience of being in a funk and then subsequently creating alignment, I can tell you firsthand that it's absolutely *not* worth it. The freedom and fulfillment you gain from actively pursuing and achieving alignment in your purpose are transformative. It's worth striving for, and when you find it, it changes your entire outlook on life.

If changing roles isn't immediately feasible, consider other ways to fulfill the purpose formula outside of your primary work. Think about starting a side hustle where you can use your skills in a way that brings you joy. Volunteering for causes you're passionate about can bring you both a positive environment and a real sense of purpose. And joining groups or communities that match your interests is a great way to dive into activities you care about and connect with people who share your passions.

Here's the bottom line: To live a truly fulfilling life, you need to incorporate an outlet where you can use your skills, doing something you enjoy in an ideal environment. Whether it's through your job, volunteering, a side hustle, or another avenue, making sure you have this in your life is essential.

How do you know if you are in a funk?

If you're feeling a lack of fulfillment, whether it's from your job or your outside interests or commitments, and if you're struggling to see how your daily tasks connect with your bigger goals or values, you might be in a funk. This persistent sense of unhappiness, even when you've achieved or made progress, is a clear sign that something's not right.

What does pursuing alignment look like?

Pursuing alignment begins with a decision to explore which parts of the STEP formula might be missing in your life. It's this decision to dig deeper and understand what's out of alignment that sparks momentum toward making meaningful changes. By acknowledging which elements of Skills, True Enjoyment, and Environment are lacking, you set the stage for taking actionable steps. This commitment to self-discovery and improvement initiates the journey toward greater fulfillment and alignment.

Your next best step:

Your next best step is diving into the STEP formula—Skills, True Enjoyment, and Environment—to figure out which part might be missing in a particular area of your life (e.g., your job, your side hustle, or volunteering). By identifying what's lacking and why, you can make targeted changes to get closer to alignment. This process involves recognizing where things are out of sync and taking proactive steps to address those gaps, ultimately leading to a greater sense of fulfillment and purpose.

Part 3 Alignment in Your Purpose

Additional Resources to Take Your Next Best Step

Explore the STEP Formula™—focusing on aligning your Skills, True Enjoyment, Environment, and Purpose—to design a fulfilling and purposeful life. Visit the Part 3 page for exercises, inspiration, and tools to help you pivot out of the funk and into your soul-aligned purpose.

Scan the QR code below to learn more or
connect with Molly for guidance on your journey.

In Conclusion

Your Next Best Step Toward a Life of Alignment

You've made it to the end of *What the Funk?!* I'm so proud of you for sticking with me on this journey. It hasn't always been easy—digging deep, getting honest with ourselves, and facing the places where we've been out of alignment takes real courage. But here's the thing: the fact that you're here, reading these final pages, shows that you're ready for something different. You're ready to stop settling for "fine" and start creating a life that feels truly aligned with who you are and what you want.

Throughout this book, we've talked about building self-awareness, embracing small shifts, and taking one intentional step after another. It's not about making a perfect plan or waiting for the right moment—it's about deciding, right here and now, to move forward with what you have, exactly as you are. You don't need to overhaul everything to see a change. Transformation happens one decision at a time, and it builds momentum the more you trust yourself and lean into the process.

So, where do you go from here? You take your next best step. It might be something small—choosing to drink more water, taking five minutes for a gratitude practice, or finally listening to that inner voice that's been whispering about a dream you've put on hold. It might be something bigger—reaching out for support, setting a boundary, or making a decision you've been avoiding. Whatever it is, know that it's enough. Each step you take toward alignment is a victory, no matter how small it may seem.

Remember, alignment isn't a destination you reach once and for all. It's a process, a practice, and a journey. It's about tuning in, adjusting as you go, and staying open to what feels right for you. And yes, there will be moments when you get off track—we all do. When that happens, instead of beating yourself up, I want you to pause, breathe, and ask yourself: *What's my next best step?* That simple question will always guide you back toward your true self.

As you close this book, I want you to carry this with you: You are capable of creating a life that feels aligned, authentic, and full of joy. You already have everything you need within you. Trust yourself. Honor what matters to you. And take it one step at a time. This is your journey, and I am cheering you on every step of the way.

Now, go out there and live a life that feels *truly* aligned. You've got this.

About the Author

Having been described as the female "Ted Lasso", Molly approaches life with a combination of grit and positivity... hence her personal moniker #mollypositivepants. She is deeply committed to her own personal growth, the potential of the people around her, and the success of the companies she leads.

In March of 2019, she made a game-changing decision that altered the trajectory of her life: she decided to finally focus on her health. This shift not only transformed her own life but also revealed her purpose: to empower others to rise above self-imposed limits, cultivate lasting health, and fully step into a life where negative thoughts and emotional baggage no longer hold them back.

Molly is the founder of Next Best Step LLC and the creator of the Next Best Step Daily Journal. She's also a monthly columnist for FORCE Magazine and a contributing author in the international best-seller The Voices of 100 Women Anthology.

LinkedIn: https://www.linkedin.com/in/molly-smith-24345712/
Facebook: https://www.facebook.com/molly.m.smith.90
Instagram: https://www.instagram.com/molly.positivepants/

Other Publications by Molly Smith

The Next Best Step Journal

Are You Ready to Get Out of Your Funk and Step Into Alignment?

Life can feel overwhelming sometimes like you're stuck in a cycle of doubt, stress, or simply feeling "off." That's why I created the *Next Best Step Journal*. This isn't just another journal; it's a resource born from real struggles, designed to help you:

- **Rediscover Gratitude**: Shift your mindset by acknowledging life's blessings and envisioning future dreams as if they've already come true.
- **Build Momentum**: Focus on your next best step and make progress toward goals that excite you.
- **Connect with Your Emotions**: Use guided prompts to identify and honor your feelings, creating space for clarity and freedom.

Each page is thoughtfully designed to help you navigate life's challenges, unlock personal growth, and embrace transformation—one intentional step at a time.

Why wait for the life you want? Start creating it today!

Get your copy of the *Next Best Step Journal* on Amazon today and take the first step toward a more aligned, joyful life.